HAL LEONARD *More* EASY POP BASS LINES

BASS METHOD
Supplement to Any Bass Method

AUDIO ACCESS INCLUDED

T0055425

INTRODUCTION

Welcome to *More Easy Pop Bass Lines*, a collection of 20 pop and rock favorites arranged for easy bass. If you're a beginning to intermediate-level bassist, you've come to the right place; these well-known songs will have you playing, reading, and enjoying music in no time!

This book can be used on its own or as a supplement to the *Hal Leonard Bass Method* or any other beginning to intermediate-level bass method. The songs are arranged in order of difficulty. Each bass line is presented in an easy-to-read format—including lyrics to help you follow along and chords for optional accompaniment (by your teacher, if you have one).

USING THE AUDIO

More *Easy Pop Bass Lines* is available as a book/audio package so you can practice playing with a real band. Each song begins with a full (or partial) measure of clicks, which sets the tempo and prepares you for playing along.

PLAYBACK+
Speed • Pitch • Balance • Loop

To access audio visit:
www.halleonard.com/mylibrary

1800-0876-6006-1521

ISBN: 978-0-634-07352-6

Visit Hal Leonard Online at
www.halleonard.com

Contact Us:
Hal Leonard
7777 West Bluemound Road
Milwaukee, WI 53213
Email: info@halleonard.com

In Europe contact:
Hal Leonard Europe Limited
Distribution Centre, Newmarket Road
Bury St Edmunds, Suffolk, IP33 3YB
Email: info@halleonardeurope.com

In Australia contact:
Hal Leonard Australia Pty. Ltd.
4 Lentara Court
Cheltenham, Victoria, 3192 Australia
Email: info@halleonard.com.au

SONG STRUCTURE

The songs in this book have different sections, which may or may not include the following:

Intro
This is usually a short instrumental section that "introduces" the song at the beginning.

Verse
This is one of the main sections of a song and conveys most of the storyline. A song usually has several verses, all with the same music but each with different lyrics.

Chorus
This is often the most memorable section of a song. Unlike the verse, the chorus usually has the same lyrics every time it repeats.

Bridge
This section is a break from the rest of the song, often having a very different chord progression and feel.

Solo
This is an instrumental section, often played over the verse or chorus structure.

Outro
Similar to an intro, this section brings the song to an end.

ENDINGS & REPEATS

Many of the songs have some new symbols that you must understand before playing. Each of these represents a different type of ending.

1st and 2nd Endings
These are indicated by brackets and numbers. The first time through a song section, play the first ending and then repeat. The second time through, skip the first ending, and play through the second ending.

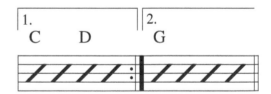

D.S.
This means "Dal Segno" or "from the sign." When you see this abbreviation above the staff, find the sign (𝄋) earlier in the song and resume playing from that point.

al Coda
This means "to the Coda," a concluding section in the song. If you see the words "D.S. al Coda," return to the sign (𝄋) earlier in the song and play until you see the words "To Coda," then skip to the Coda at the end of the song, indicated by the symbol: ⊕.

al Fine
This means "to the end." If you see the words "D.S. al Fine," return to the sign (𝄋) earlier in the song and play until you see the word "Fine."

D.C.
This means "Da Capo" or "from the head." When you see this abbreviation above the staff, return to the beginning (or "head") of the song and resume playing.

CONTENTS

ROCK AND ROLL ALL NITE

Words and Music by
PAUL STANLEY and GENE SIMMONS

1. You show us ev-'ry-thing you've got. _____
2. You keep on say-in' you'll be mine for a-while. _____

You keep on danc-in' and the room _____ gets hot.
You're look-in' fan-cy and I like your style.

You drive us wild; _____ we'll drive you cra -
And you drive us wild; _____ we'll drive you cra -

Dsus4 D Dsus4 D A   E

- zy. ___   You ___ say you wan - na
- zy. ___   You ___ show us ev - 'ry -

A   E

go for a spin. __ The par - ty's just be - gun; we'll
thing you've ___ got. __ Ba - by, ba - by, that's

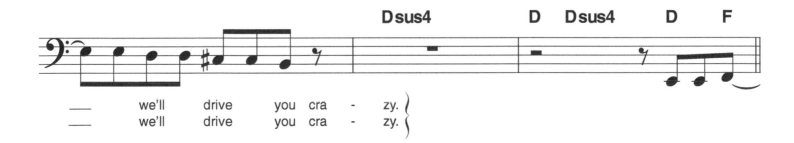

D   E

let you in.   You drive us wild; ___
quite a lot.   And you drive us wild; ___

Dsus4 D Dsus4 D F

___ we'll drive you cra - zy.
___ we'll drive you cra - zy.

Pre-Chorus

F   G

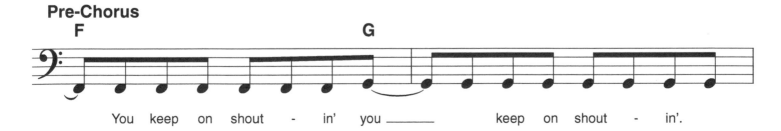

You keep on shout - in' you _____ keep on shout - in'.

Chorus

A   D

I _____ wan - na rock and roll ___ all night, __

and par-ty ev-er-y day. I wan-na

rock and roll __ all night _____ and par-ty ev-er-y day.

I wan-na rock and roll __ all night _____ and par-ty ev-er-y day.

I wan-na rock and roll __ all night _____ and par-ty ev-er-y day.

and par-ty ev-er-y day. I wan-na

Play 5 times and fade

rock and roll __ all night _____ and par-ty ev-er-y day.

MESSAGE IN A BOTTLE

Music and Lyrics by
STING

Melody:

Just a cast - a - way, ___

Intro

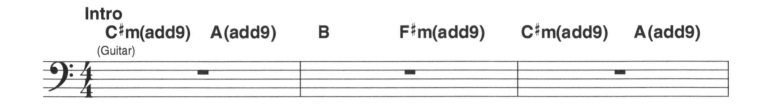

C#m(add9)   A(add9)   B   F#m(add9)   C#m(add9)   A(add9)

(Guitar)

B   F#m(add9) C#m   %Verse   A   B

1. Just a cast -
2. A year ___
3. Walked out this ___

F#m   C#m   A   B

- a - way, ___   an is - land   lost ___ at   sea, ___
___ has passed since   I wrote my   note ___
___ morn - ing, ___   I don't be - lieve ___ what   I

F#m   C#m   A   B   F#m   C#m

___ oh. ___   An - oth - er lone - ly day, ___
saw,   but I should have known this right from the
                   a hun - dred bil - lion bot - tles ___

I hope ___ that some - one gets ___ my ___ mes - sage in ___ a bot -

To Coda ⊕

- tle, ___ yeah.

Mes-sage in ___ a bot - tle, ___ yeah.

Mes-sage in ___ a bot - tle, ___ yeah.

A   C#m   A

Mes - sage in ___ a bot - tle, ___ yeah.

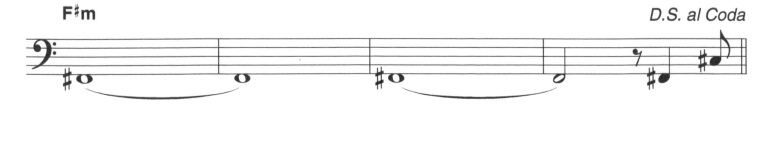

F#m   D.S. al Coda

Coda

C#m   A   C#m

Mes-sage in ___ a bot - tle, ___

A   C#m   A

mes-sage in ___ a bot - tle, ___

C#m   A   C#m

mes-sage in ___ a bot -

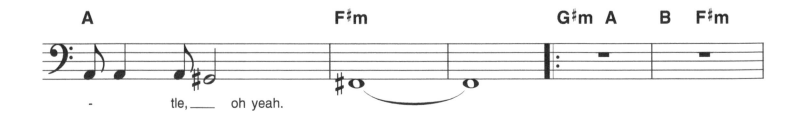

A   F#m   G#m A   B F#m

- tle, ___ oh yeah.

Outro   *Repeat and fade*

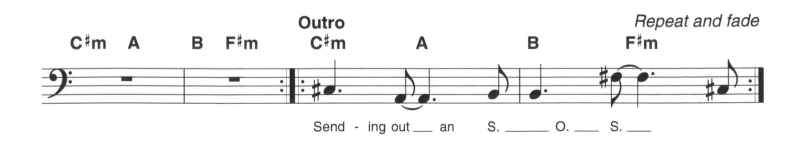

C#m A   B F#m   C#m   A   B   F#m

Send - ing out ___ an S. ___ O. ___ S. ___

PARANOID

Words and Music by ANTHONY IOMMI,
JOHN OSBOURNE, WILLIAM WARD and TERENCE BUTLER

Melody:

Fin - ished with my wom - an...

1. Fin - ished with my wom - an 'cause she
2. All day long I think of things but
3. I need some - one to show me the

could not help me with my mind.____
noth - ing seems to sat - is - fy.
things in life that I ____ can't find.

Peo - ple think I'm in - sane be - cause I
Think I'll lose my mind if I don't find
I can't see the things that make true hap -

am frown - ing all the time.
some - thing to pac - i - fy.
- pi - ness I must be blind.

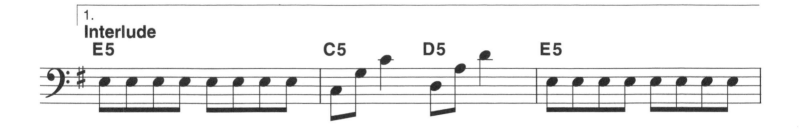

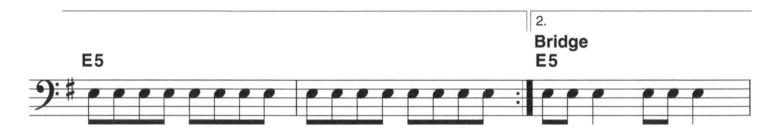

Can you help me   oc - cu - py my

brain?_____   Whoa _____   yeah. _____

Interlude

D.S. al Coda

⊕ *Coda*
Guitar Solo

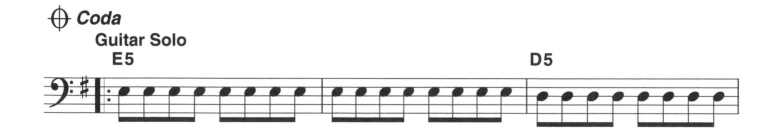

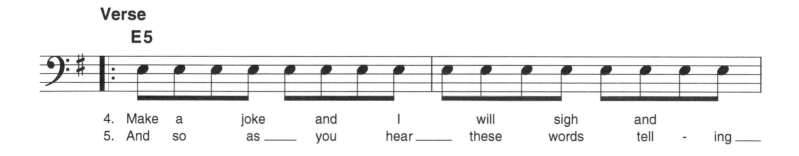

Verse

4. Make a joke and I will sigh and
5. And so as ___ you hear ___ these words tell - ing ___

you will laugh and I ___ will cry. Hap-pi - ness I can -
___ you now ___ of ___ my state; I tell you ___ to en -

- not feel ___ and love to me ___ is
- joy life ___ I wish I could ___ but

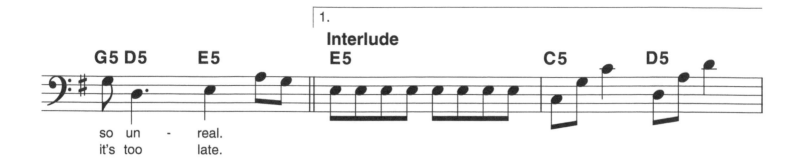

so un - real.
it's too late.

NO EXCUSES

Written by
JERRY CANTRELL

It's al - right. _____

Intro

(Drums) 4 **Badd4**

%Verse
Badd4

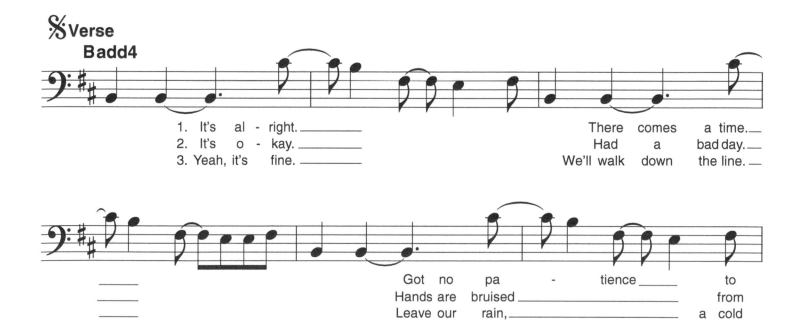

1. It's al - right. _____ There comes a time. _____
2. It's o - kay. _____ Had a bad day. _____
3. Yeah, it's fine. _____ We'll walk down the line. _____

_____ Got no pa - tience _____ to
_____ Hands are bruised _____ from
_____ Leave our rain, _____ a cold

search for peace___ of mind. _____   Lay-in' low. _
break - ing rocks___ all day. _____   Drained and blue, _
trade for warm___ sun - shine. _____   You my friend _

_____   Want to take it slow. _____
           I bleed for you. _____
           I will de - fend. _____

To Coda ⊕

    No more hid - ing___ or dis - guis - ing truths I've sold. _
You think it's fun - ny___ well, you're drown - ing in it too. _
And if we change, _____ well, I love you an - y - way. _

Chorus
G6   **Aadd2**

_____   Ev-'ry day ___ it's some - thing, hits ___

Badd4   **Aadd2** **G6**   **Aadd2**

___ me all so cold. ___   You find me sit - tin' by___

E

___ my - self, ___ no ex - cus - es, then I know. ___

Interlude

Guitar Solo

D.S. al Coda

Coda

Chorus

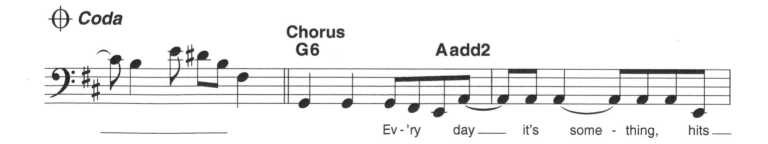

Ev-'ry day ___ it's some-thing, hits ___

_me all so ___ cold. ___   You find me sit-tin' by___

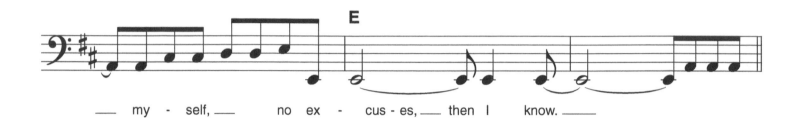

_my - self, ___   no ex - cus - es, ___ then I   know. ___

Outro
Badd4

Drums tacet

JAMMING

Words and Music by
BOB MARLEY

Melody:

We're jam-ming.

Intro

Bm7   E9

G   F#m   1.   2.

Ooo,_ yeah.   Al - right.   We're

Chorus

Bm   E7   G   F#m

jam-ming.   I wan - na jam it with you._

Bm   E7

_   We're jam - ming,   jam - ming,   and I

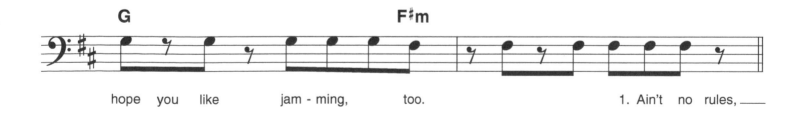

G   F#m

hope you like jam - ming, too.   1. Ain't no rules,_

Verse

___ ain't no vow, we can do it an-y-how. ___
bul-lets can stop us now, we nei - ther beg nor we won't bow.

I and I will see you through. ___ 'Cause ev - er - y -
Nei - ther can be bought nor sold. ___ We

day we pay the price. We are the liv - ing sac - ri - fice,
all de - fend the right, Jah Jah child - ren must u - nite, well,

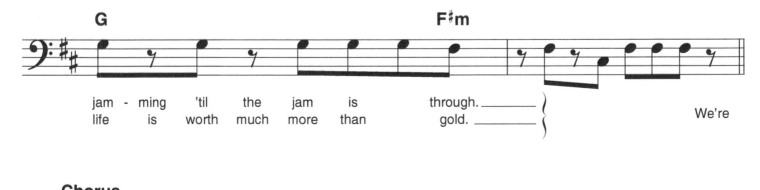

jam - ming 'til the jam is through. ___ We're
life is worth much more than gold. ___

Chorus

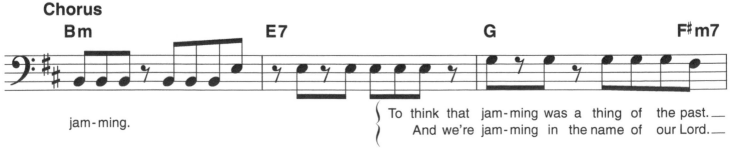

jam-ming.

To think that jam - ming was a thing of the past. ___
And we're jam - ming in the name of our Lord. ___

Bm | E7

We're jam-ming, and I we're

G | F♯m7 | **Interlude** Bm

hope this jam is gon-na last. 2. No Ho - ly
jam-ming right straight from yard.

Em | Bm | Em

Mount Zi - on, ho - ly Mount Zi - on,

Bm

Jah sit-teth in Mount Zi - on and rules___ all ___ cre-a-tion. Yeah, we're,

Chorus
Bm | E7

we're jam-ming, Bop - chu - wah - wah -

STAND BY ME

Words and Music by
BEN E. KING, JERRY LEIBER and MIKE STOLLER

Melody:

When the night ___

Intro

1. When the night ___

Verse

___ has come ___ and the land is dark ___
___ be a - fraid, no ___ I ___ won't be a -

___ and the moon ___ is the on - ly ___ light ___ we'll
fraid. Just as long ___ as you stand, ___ stand by ___

see.

_____ me.   So,   2. No I won't _____ dar - ling,   dar - ling

Chorus

stand _____   by   me. _____   Oh, _____   stand _____   by _____

me. _____   Oh,   stand, _____   stand by ___ me, _____

Guitar Solo

stand   by ___ me. ___

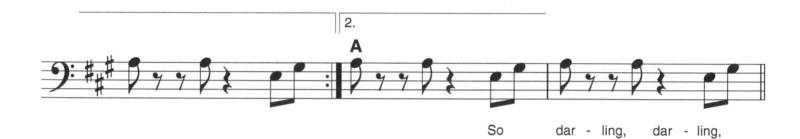

So dar - ling, dar - ling,

Chorus

stand   by me _____   oh, _____ stand   by

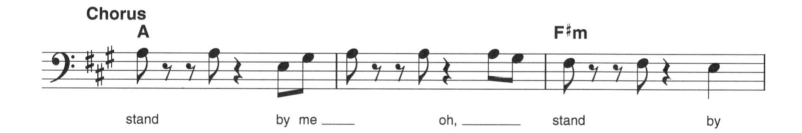

me.   Oh, stand,   stand by ____ me, _____

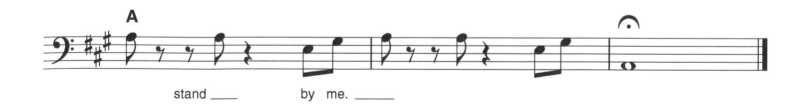

stand _____   by me. _____

DAY TRIPPER

Words and Music by
JOHN LENNON and PAUL McCARTNEY

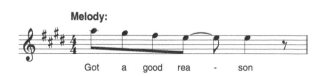

Melody:

Got a good rea - son

Intro

N.C.
(Guitar)

E

Verse

E

1. Got   a   good rea - son   for
2. She's a   big   teas - er.
3. Tried ____ to   please ____ her.

tak - ing   the   eas - y   way   out. ____
She   took   me   half ____ the   way   there. ____
She   on - ly played ____ one   night   stands. ____

A

Got a good rea - son

She's a big teas - er.

Tried to please her.

E

tak - ing the eas - y way out now.

She took me half the way there now.

She on - ly played one night stands, now.

She was a

Chorus

F#

day trip-per,

1., 2. one way tick - et, yeah.

3. Sun-day driv - er, yeah.

A   **G#**

It took me so long to find out

1., 3.

To Coda   **Interlude**

C#   **B**   **N.C.**

and I found out.

E

27

Outro

Day   trip - per.

Day   trip - per,   yeah._____

Day   trip - per.

Day   trip - per,   yeah._____

CRAZY TRAIN

Words and Music by
OZZY OSBOURNE, RANDY RHOADS and BOB DAISLEY

Melody:

Cra - zy,

Intro

All aboard ha, ha, ha,...

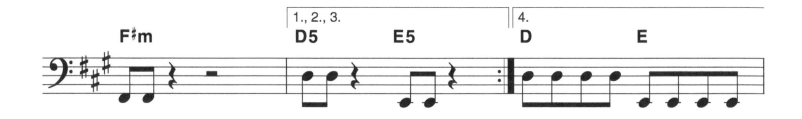

1. Cra - zy,

but that's how it goes._____

Mil-lions of peo - ple liv - ing as foes._____

Chorus

Men - tal wounds still scream - ing,
Men - tal wounds not heal - ing,

driv - ing me in - sane._____
who and what's to blame?_____

I'm go - ing off___ the rails ___

_____ on a cra - zy train.___

I'm

go - ing off___ the rails_____ on a cra - zy train._____

To Coda ⊕

Bridge

I know that things are go - ing wrong for me.___

You've got - ta lis - ten to my

Guitar Solo

words,_____ yeah,_____ yeah._____

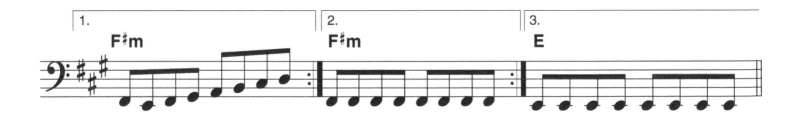

1.

2.

3.

1.

2. *D.S. al Coda*

✛ *Coda*

Repeat and fade

34

Ramblin' Man

Words and Music by
DICKEY BETTS

Melody:

Lord, I was born a ram - blin' man.

Intro

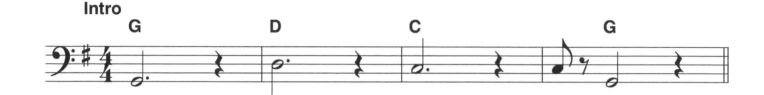

G   D   C   G

Chorus

G   F   C   G

Lord I was born a ram - blin' man.

C

Try'n' to make a liv - in' and do - in' the best I

D6   D   C

can.   An' when it's time for

G   Em   C

leav - in' I hope you'll un - der - stand,

Chorus

Lord, I ____ was born____ a ram - blin'

man. _____ Try'n' to make a liv - ing and

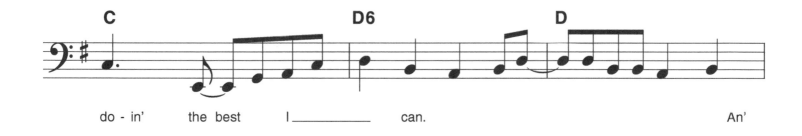

do - in' the best I _____ can. An'

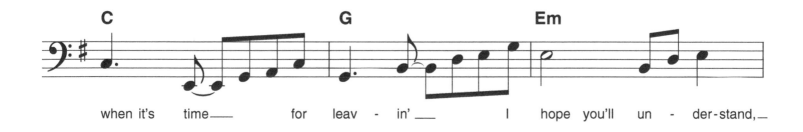

when it's time___ for leav - in' ___ I hope you'll un - der-stand, __

To Coda

__ that I was born____ a ram - blin'

Interlude

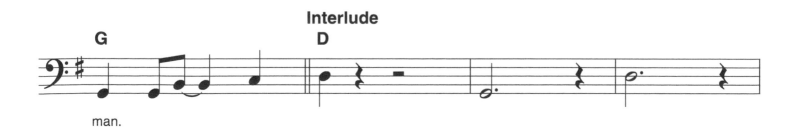

man.

Guitar Solo

D.S. al Coda

2. I'm

⊕ Coda

Outro-Chorus

man.   Lord, I ___ was born ___

Repeat and fade

___ a ram - blin' man. _____

JET AIRLINER

Words and Music by
PAUL PENA

Melody:

Leav-in' on out ___ on the road. ___

Intro

C5

Verse

C5   F5   C5   F5

1. Leav - in' on ___ out _____ on the road. ___
2. Good - bye to all _____ my friends at home, good - bye _____
3. Touch - in' down in New En - gland town, ___

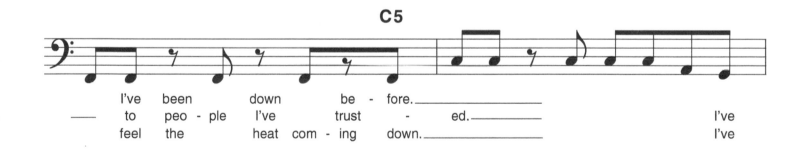

C5

I've been down be - fore. _____
___ to peo - ple I've trust - ed. _____ I've
feel the heat com - ing down. _____ I've

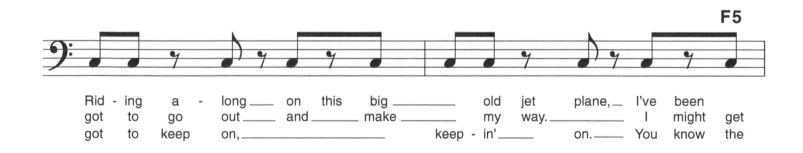

F5

Rid - ing a - long ___ on this big _____ old jet plane, ___ I've been
got to go out ___ and ___ make _____ my way. ___ I might get
got to keep on, _____ keep - in' ___ on. ___ You know the

think - in' a - bout_____ my home._____ But my love__
rich you know, I might get__ bust - ed.____ But my
big wheel_____ keeps a spin - ning a - round. And I'm

__ light seems _____ so far _____ a - way, __ and I ____
heart keeps call - ing me back - wards,_____ as I
go - ing with some hes - i - ta - tion._____ You know that

B♭5   **F5**   **C5**

feel like it's all__ been done.__ some - bod -y's try - in'_ to make_
get on the sev - en - o - sev - en. Rid - in', I got
I can sure - ly see, that I don't ____ want _ to__ get _

B♭5   **F5**

__ me stay. You know I've got to be mov - in'
tears in my eyes. You know you've got to go through hell be - fore you
__ caught __ up in an-y of that funk - y kicks go - in' down_

𝄉 **Chorus**

C5   **B♭5**   **F5**

on.   Oh. _____ Big ol' jet __ air - lin -
get to heav - en.
__ in the cit - y.

C5   **B♭5**   **F5**   **C5**

- er, __ don't __ car - ry me too far a - way. __ Oh, __

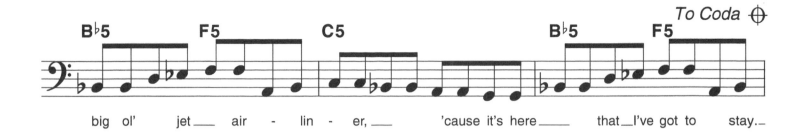

big ol' jet ___ air - lin - er, ___ 'cause it's here ___ that __ I've got to stay. _

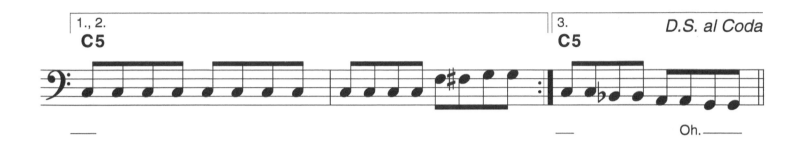

__ — Oh. __

__ — Yeah, yeah, yeah, yeah! __ Big ol' jet __ air - lin -

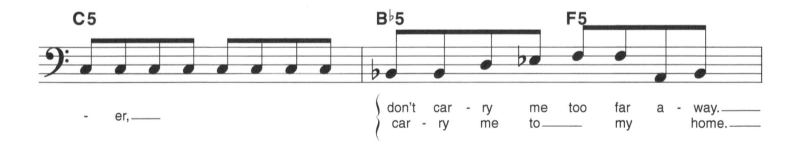

- er, __

don't car - ry me too far a - way. __
car - ry me to __ my home. __

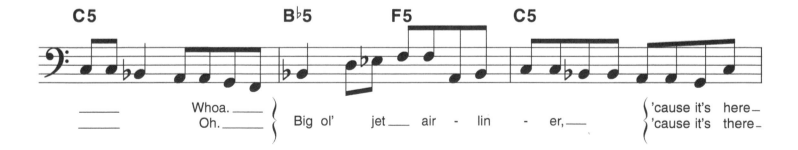

___ Whoa. __
___ Oh. __

Big ol' jet __ air - lin - er, __

'cause it's here _
'cause it's there _

__ that __ I've got to stay. __
__ that ___ I be - long. __

Oh. __

I HEARD IT THROUGH THE GRAPEVINE

Words and Music by
NORMAN J. WHITFIELD and BARRETT STRONG

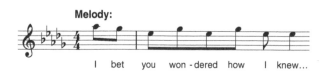

Melody:

I bet you won-dered how I knew...

Intro

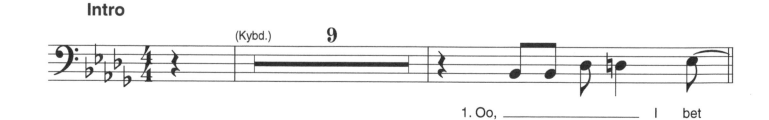

(Kybd.) **9**

1. Oo, _____ I bet

Verse

E♭m ... B♭

you, won-dered how I knew 'bout your plans ___

A♭9 ... E♭m

___ to make me blue with some oth-er guy ___ you knew be-fore.

B♭ ... A♭9 ... Cm7

Be-tween the two of us guys, ___ you know I love you more. It took me by sur-

A♭ ... Cm7/E♭ ... A♭

prise, ___ I must say ___ when I found ___ out ___ yes-ter-day. ___

43

RHIANNON

Words and Music by
STEVIE NICKS

Am

non. _____ Rhi - an -

Am

\- non. _____ Rhi -

D.S. al Coda
(take 2nd ending)

F

an - non. ___

⊕ *Coda*

Outro-Chorus

Am **F**

Rhi - an -

Am

\- non._____

Repeat and fade

F

Rhi - an -

47

Summer of '69

Words and Music by
BRYAN ADAMS and JIM VALLANCE

*Note played above the 12th fret.

Man,— we were kill-in' time.— We were young and rest-less, we need-ed to un-wind. I guess noth-in' can last — for - ev - er, for - ev - er.— No!

Yeah!

Back in the sum - mer of six - ty - nine.—

Uh, huh.— It was the sum-mer of

YOU SHOOK ME

Written by
WILLIE DIXON and J. B. LENOIR

Harmonica Solo

Guitar Solo

3. You_ know you

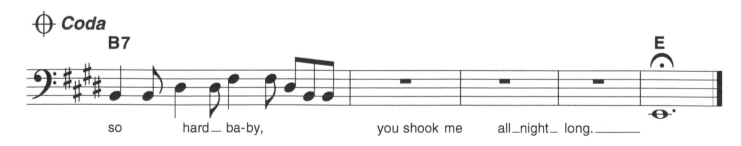

so   hard_ ba-by,   you shook me   all_night_ long._____

Blue Suede Shoes

Words and Music by
CARL LEE PERKINS

wan - na do. _____ But uh uh hon - ey lay off _____ of my shoes. And don't

B♭7   **F**

_____ you step on my blue suede shoes. You can

C9   **F**

do an - y - thing _____ but lay off _____ of my blue _ suede shoes.

F

Blue, blue, blue suede shoes. Blue, blue,

B♭7

blue suede shoes, yeah! Blue, blue, blue suede shoes, ba - by.

F   **C7**

Blue, blue, blue suede shoes. You could do an - y - thing _ but lay off _

F   **F6**

_ of my blue suede shoes.

DON'T BE CRUEL
(TO A HEART THAT'S TRUE)

Words and Music by
OTIS BLACKWELL and ELVIS PRESLEY

true.   Why should we be a - part   I

real - ly love you ba - by cross my heart._____ Don't be cruel_____

____ to a heart that's true._____ Don't be cruel_____

____ to a heart that's true.   I don't want no oth - er

love,   ba - by, it's just you I'm think - ing of._____

LAY DOWN SALLY

Words and Music by ERIC CLAPTON,
MARCY LEVY and GEORGE TERRY

There is noth - ing that ___ is wrong ___

Intro

Country Shuffle

𝄋 Verse

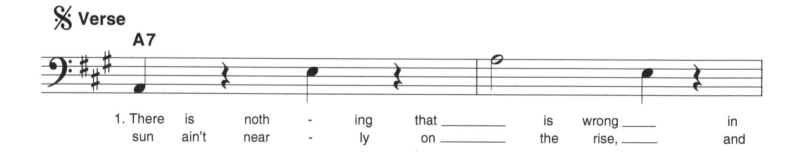

1. There is noth - ing that _____ is wrong _____ in
sun ain't near - ly on _____ the rise, _____ and

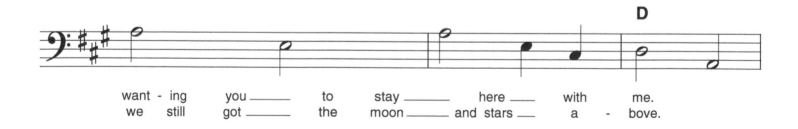

want - ing you _____ to stay _____ here _____ with me.
we still got _____ the moon _____ and stars _____ a - bove.

I know you've got _____ some - where _____ to go, _____ but
Un - der - neath _____ the vel - vet skies,

won't you make _____ your - self _____ at home _____ and stay with me? _____
love is all _____ that mat - ters. Won't _____ you stay with me? _____

And don't you ev - er leave. _____

Lay down Sal -

- ly, and rest here in _____ my arms. _____

Don't you _____ think _____ you want _____ some - one _____ to talk _____

BAD, BAD LEROY BROWN

Words and Music by
JIM CROCE

Outro-Chorus

Le - roy looked __ like a jig - saw puz - zle with a cou - ple of piec - es gone. And it's bad, ____ bad Le - roy Brown, __ bad-dest man __ in the whole __ damn town. __ Bad - der than a old King Kong, ____ mean - er than a junk-yard dog. __ And he's bad, ____ Le - roy Brown, ____ bad-dest man __ in the whole __ damn __ town. __ Bad-der than a old King Kong, ____ mean - er than a junk-yard dog. ____ Yeah, he was bad-der than a old King Kong, ____ mean - er than a junk-yard dog. ____

PRIDE AND JOY

Written by
STEVIE RAY VAUGHAN

Melody:

Well you've heard a - bout love...

Intro

Blues Shuffle

(Guitar)

Verse

1. Well you've hear a-bout love giv-in' sight __ to the blind. __

My ba-by's lov-in' 'cause the sun to shine. __ She's my

sweet lit-tle thing. __ She's my pride and joy. __

She's my sweet lit-tle ba - by, I'm __ her __ lit-tle lov-er

boy. _____ 2. Yeah, I

Verse

love my ba-by my heart and __ soul. __ Love like ours won't

nev - er grow___ old. She's my sweet lit - tle thing. __

She's my pride and joy. _____

She's my sweet lit-tle ba - by I'm ___ her ___ lit - tle lov - er

boy. _____   3. Yeah I love my la - dy she's

long and a lean. __   You mess with her, you'll see a

man get - tin' mean. ___ She's my sweet lit - tle thing. ___

She's my pride and joy. ___ She's my

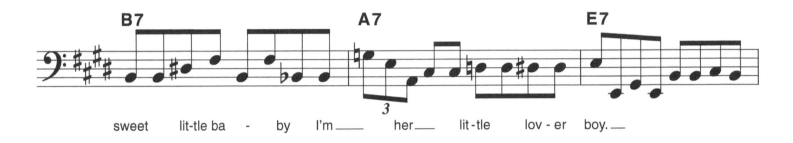

sweet lit-tle ba - by I'm ___ her ___ lit -tle lov - er boy. ___

Guitar Solo

MY GENERATION

Words and Music by
PETER TOWNSHEND

3. Why don't _you all   f-f - fade____ a-way._____   Yeah,

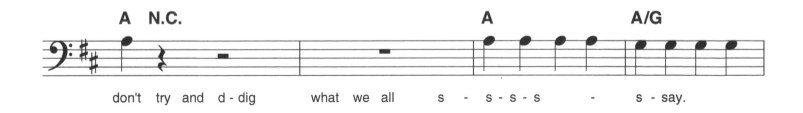

don't try and d-dig   what we all   s - s-s-s - s-say.

Not try-in' to cause big sen - sa - tion,   just

talk - in' 'bout my g-gen - er-a - tion._____   Ba - by, my __ gen-er-a-

Chorus

- tion, ___   this is my __ gen-er - a - tion, ba - by._____

___   My,   my,   ge - gen - er -

a - tion. My,   my   ooh, my,   my.

4. Peo - ple   try   to   put us d - down_____

HAL LEONARD BASS METHOD

METHOD BOOKS

by Ed Friedland

BOOK 1 - 2ND EDITION

Book 1 teaches: tuning; playing position; musical symbols; notes within the first five frets; common bass lines, patterns and rhythms; rhythms through eighth notes; playing tips and techniques; more than 100 great songs, riffs and examples; and more! The audio includes 44 full-band tracks for demonstration or play-along.

00695067 Book Only...................................$9.99
00695068 Book/Online Audio...........................$14.99
01100122 Deluxe - Book/Online Audio/Video......$19.99

BOOK 2 - 2ND EDITION

Book 2 continues where Book 1 left off and teaches: the box shape; moveable boxes; notes in fifth position; major and minor scales; the classic blues line; the shuffle rhythm; tablature; and more!

00695069 Book Only...................................$9.99
00695070 Book/Online Audio...........................$14.99

BOOK 3 - 2ND EDITION

With the third book, progressing students will learn more great songs, riffs and examples; sixteenth notes; playing off chord symbols; slap and pop techniques; hammer-ons and pull-offs; playing different styles and grooves; and more.

00695071 Book Only...................................$9.99
00695072 Book/Online Audio...........................$14.99

COMPOSITE - 2ND EDITION

This money-saving edition contains Books 1, 2 and 3.

00695073 Book Only...................................$19.99
00695074 Book/Online Audio...........................$27.99

DVD

Play your favorite songs in no time with this DVD! Covers: tuning, notes in first through third position, rhythms through eighth notes, fingerstyle and pick playing, 4/4 and 3/4 time, and more! Includes 6 full songs and on-screen music notation. 68 minutes.

00695849 DVD $19.95

BASS FOR KIDS

by Chad Johnson

Bass for Kids is a fun, easy course that teaches children to play bass guitar faster than ever before. Popular songs such as "Crazy Train," "Every Breath You Take," "A Hard Day's Night" and "Wild Thing" keep kids motivated, and the clean, simple page layouts ensure their attention remains focused on one concept at a time.

00696449 Book/Online Audio $14.99

REFERENCE BOOKS

BASS SCALE FINDER

by Chad Johnson

Learn to use the entire fretboard with the *Bass Scale Finder*. This book contains over 1,300 scale diagrams for the most important 17 scale types.

00695781 6" x 9" Edition......................$9.99
00695778 9" x 12" Edition....................$10.99

BASS ARPEGGIO FINDER

by Chad Johnson

This extensive reference guide lays out over 1,300 arpeggio shapes. 28 different qualities are covered for each key, and each quality is presented in four different shapes.

00695817 6" x 9" Edition......................$9.99
00695816 9" x 12" Edition....................$9.99

MUSIC THEORY FOR BASSISTS

by Sean Malone

Acclaimed bassist and composer Sean Malone will explain the written language of music, using easy-to-understand terms and concepts, diagrams, and much more. The audio provides 96 tracks of examples, demonstrations, and play-alongs.

00695756 Book/Online Audio $19.99

STYLE BOOKS

BASS LICKS

by Ed Friedland

This comprehensive supplement to any bass method will help students learn over 200 great bass licks, lines and grooves in many rhythmic styles. *Bass Licks* illustrates how simple melodic patterns can become the springboard for group improvisation or the foundation of a song.

00696035 Book/Online Audio $15.99

BASS LINES

by Matt Scharfglass

500 expertly written bass lines, riffs and fills in a wide variety of musical genres are included in this comprehensive collection to help players expand their bass vocabulary. The examples cover many tempos, keys and feels, and include easy bass lines for beginners on up to advanced riffs for more experienced bassists.

00148194 Book/Online Audio $22.99

BLUES BASS

by Ed Friedland

Learn to play studying the songs of B.B. King, Stevie Ray Vaughan, Muddy Waters, Albert King, the Allman Brothers, T-Bone Walker, and many more. Learn riffs from blues classics including: Born Under a Bad Sign • Hideaway • Hoochie Coochie Man • Killing Floor • Pride and Joy • Sweet Home Chicago • The Thrill Is Gone • and more.

00695870 Book/Online Audio $17.99

COUNTRY BASS

by Glenn Letsch

21 songs, including: Act Naturally • Boot Scootin' Boogie • Crazy • Honky Tonk Man • Love You Out Loud • Luckenbach, Texas (Back to the Basics of Love) • No One Else on Earth • Ring of Fire • Southern Nights • Streets of Bakersfield • Whose Bed Have Your Boots Been Under? • and more.

00695928 Book/Online Audio $22.99

FRETLESS BASS

by Chris Kringel

18 songs, including: Bad Love • Continuum • Even Flow • Everytime You Go Away • Hocus Pocus • I Could Die for You • Jelly Roll • King of Pain • Kiss of Life • Lady in Red • Tears in Heaven • Very Early • What I Am • White Room • more.

00695850...$22.99

FUNK BASS

by Chris Kringel

This is your complete guide to learning the basics of grooving and soloing funk bass. Songs include: Can't Stop • I'll Take You There • Let's Groove • Stay • What Is Hip • and more.

00695792 Book/Online Audio..............$22.99

R&B BASS

by Glenn Letsch

This book/audio pack uses actual classic R&B, Motown, soul and funk songs to teach you how to groove in the style of James Jamerson, Bootsy Collins, Bob Babbitt, and many others. The 19 songs include: For Once in My Life • Knock on Wood • Mustang Sally • Respect • Soul Man • Stand by Me • and more.

00695823 Book/Online Audio $19.99

ROCK BASS

by Sean Malone

This book/audio pack uses songs from a myriad of rock genres to teach the key elements of rock bass. Includes: Another One Bites the Dust • Beast of Burden • Money • Roxanne • Smells like Teen Spirit • and more.

00695801 Book/Online Audio..............$22.99

SUPPLEMENTARY SONGBOOKS

These great songbooks correlate with Books 1-3 of the *Hal Leonard Bass Method*, giving students great songs to play while they're still learning! The audio tracks include great accompaniment and demo tracks.

EASY POP BASS LINES

20 great songs that students in Book 1 can master. Includes: Come as You Are • Crossfire • Great Balls of Fire • Imagine • Surfin' U.S.A. • Takin' Care of Business • Wild Thing • and more.

00695809 Book/Online Audio..............$16.99

MORE EASY POP BASS LINES

20 great songs for Level 2 students. Includes: Bad, Bad Leroy Brown • Crazy Train • I Heard It Through the Grapevine • My Generation • Pride and Joy • Ramblin' Man • Summer of '69 • and more.

00695819 Book Only...........................$14.99
00695818 Book/Online Audio..............$16.99

EVEN MORE EASY POP BASS LINES

20 great songs for Level 3 students, including: ABC • Another One Bites the Dust • Brick House • Come Together • Higher Ground • Iron Man • The Joker • Sweet Emotion • Under Pressure • more.

00695821 Book.................................$14.99
00695820 Book/Online Audio..............$16.99

Visit Hal Leonard online at
www.halleonard.com

Prices, contents and availability subject to change without notice.
Some products may not be available outside of U.S.A.

BASS BUILDERS

A series of technique book/audio packages created for the purposeful building and development of your chops. Each volume is written by an expert in that particular technique. And with the inclusion of audio, the added dimension of hearing exactly how to play particular grooves and techniques make these truly like private lessons.

BASS FOR BEGINNERS
by Glenn Letsch
00695099 Book/CD Pack.........................$19.95

BASS GROOVES
by Jon Liebman
00696028 Book/Online Audio $19.99

BASS IMPROVISATION
by Ed Friedland
00695164 Book/Online Audio $19.99

BLUES BASS
by Jon Liebman
00695235 Book/Online Audio $19.99

BUILDING WALKING BASS LINES
by Ed Friedland
00695008 Book/Online Audio $19.99

**RON CARTER –
BUILDING JAZZ BASS LINES**
00841240 Book/Online Audio $19.99

DICTIONARY OF BASS GROOVES
by Sean Malone
00695266 Book/Online Audio $14.95

EXPANDING WALKING BASS LINES
by Ed Friedland
00695026 Book/Online Audio $19.99

FINGERBOARD HARMONY FOR BASS
by Gary Willis
00695043 Book/Online Audio $17.99

FUNK BASS
by Jon Liebman
00699348 Book/Online Audio $19.99

FUNK/FUSION BASS
by Jon Liebman
00696553 Book/Online Audio $24.99

HIP-HOP BASS
by Josquin des Prés
00695589 Book/Online Audio $15.99

JAZZ BASS
by Ed Friedland
00695084 Book/Online Audio $17.99

**JERRY JEMMOTT –
BLUES AND RHYTHM &
BLUES BASS TECHNIQUE**
00695176 Book/CD Pack.........................$24.99

JUMP 'N' BLUES BASS
by Keith Rosier
00695292 Book/Online Audio $17.99

THE LOST ART OF COUNTRY BASS
by Keith Rosier
00695107 Book/Online Audio $19.99

PENTATONIC SCALES FOR BASS
by Ed Friedland
00696224 Book/Online Audio $19.99

REGGAE BASS
by Ed Friedland
00695163 Book/Online Audio $16.99

'70S FUNK & DISCO BASS
by Josquin des Prés
00695614 Book/Online Audio $16.99

**SIMPLIFIED SIGHT-READING
FOR BASS**
by Josquin des Prés
00695085 Book/Online Audio $17.99

6-STRING BASSICS
by David Gross
00695221 Book/Online Audio $14.99

halleonard.com

Prices, contents and availability subject to change without notice; All prices are listed in U.S. funds

Hal•Leonard® BASS PLAY-ALONG

The Bass Play-Along™ Series will help you play your favorite songs quickly and easily! Just follow the tab, listen to the audio to hear how the bass should sound, and then play-along using the separate backing tracks. The melody and lyrics are also included in the book in case you want to sing, or to simply help you follow along. The audio files are enhanced so you can adjust the recording to any tempo without changing pitch!

1. Rock
00699674 Book/Online Audio $16.99

2. R&B
00699675 Book/Online Audio $16.99

3. Songs for Beginners
00346426 Book/Online Audio $16.99

4. '90s Rock
00294992 Book/Online Audio $16.99

5. Funk
00699680 Book/Online Audio $16.99

6. Classic Rock
00699678 Book/Online Audio $17.99

8. Punk Rock
00699813 Book/CD Pack $12.95

9. Blues
00699817 Book/Online Audio $16.99

10. Jimi Hendrix – Smash Hits
00699815 Book/Online Audio $17.99

11. Country
00699818 Book/CD Pack $12.95

12. Punk Classics
00699814 Book/CD Pack $12.99

13. The Beatles
00275504 Book/Online Audio $17.99

14. Modern Rock
00699821 Book/CD Pack $14.99

15. Mainstream Rock
00699822 Book/CD Pack $14.99

16. '80s Metal
00699825 Book/CD Pack $16.99

17. Pop Metal
00699826 Book/CD Pack $14.99

18. Blues Rock
00699828 Book/CD Pack $19.99

19. Steely Dan
00700203 Book/Online Audio $17.99

20. The Police
00700270 Book/Online Audio $19.99

21. Metallica: 1983-1988
00234338 Book/Online Audio $19.99

22. Metallica: 1991-2016
00234339 Book/Online Audio $19.99

23. Pink Floyd – Dark Side of The Moon
00700847 Book/Online Audio $16.99

24. Weezer
00700960 Book/CD Pack $17.99

25. Nirvana
00701047 Book/Online Audio $17.99

26. Black Sabbath
00701180 Book/Online Audio $17.99

27. Kiss
00701181 Book/Online Audio $17.99

28. The Who
00701182 Book/Online Audio $19.99

29. Eric Clapton
00701183 Book/Online Audio $17.99

30. Early Rock
00701184 Book/CD Pack $15.99

31. The 1970s
00701185 Book/CD Pack $14.99

32. Cover Band Hits
00211598 Book/Online Audio $16.99

33. Christmas Hits
00701197 Book/CD Pack $12.99

34. Easy Songs
00701480 Book/Online Audio $17.99

35. Bob Marley
00701702 Book/Online Audio $17.99

36. Aerosmith
00701886 Book/CD Pack $14.99

37. Modern Worship
00701920 Book/Online Audio $19.99

38. Avenged Sevenfold
00702386 Book/CD Pack $16.99

39. Queen
00702387 Book/Online Audio $17.99

40. AC/DC
14041594 Book/Online Audio $17.99

41. U2
00702582 Book/Online Audio $19.99

42. Red Hot Chili Peppers
00702991 Book/Online Audio.....................................$19.99

43. Paul McCartney
00703079 Book/Online Audio $19.99

44. Megadeth
00703080 Book/CD Pack $16.99

45. Slipknot
00703201 Book/CD Pack $17.99

46. Best Bass Lines Ever
00103359 Book/Online Audio.....................................$19.99

47. Dream Theater
00111940 Book/Online Audio $24.99

48. James Brown
00117421 Book/CD Pack...$16.99

49. Eagles
00119936 Book/Online Audio $17.99

50. Jaco Pastorius
00128407 Book/Online Audio $17.99

51. Stevie Ray Vaughan
00146154 Book/CD Pack...$16.99

52. Cream
00146159 Book/Online Audio $19.99

56. Bob Seger
00275503 Book/Online Audio $16.99

57. Iron Maiden
00278398 Book/Online Audio $17.99

58. Southern Rock
00278436 Book/Online Audio $17.99

HAL•LEONARD®

Visit Hal Leonard Online at **www.halleonard.com**